# Writer's Dictionary

## Intermediate Level

This book belongs to:

_____

STECK-VAUGHN
ELEMENTARY · SECONDARY · ADULT · LIBRARY

A Harcourt Company

www.steck-vaughn.com

## Acknowledgments

**Editorial Director:** Stephanie Muller
**Senior Editor:** Amanda Sperry
**Associate Director of Design:** Cynthia Ellis
**Designer:** Alexandra Corona
**Electronic Production Artist:** Linda Reed

**Illustrations:** Terry Chicko

ISBN 0-7398-0106-6

Copyright ©2001 Steck-Vaughn Company

Printed in the United States of America

1 2 3 4 5 6 7 8 9 LB 04 03 02 01 00

# How to Use This Dictionary

To the student: This is your dictionary. It is your place to write words you have learned and words you want to remember. You may want to remember a word's spelling, or you may want to remember its meaning. The dictionary provides space for you to write words and their meanings. You may also want to draw pictures that help you remember spellings and meanings. The dictionary already has some words. You can add many others.

The front part of the dictionary has alphabet pages. Fun limericks and tongue twisters on these pages feature the letters and their sounds. Memory joggers on the alphabet pages can help you remember how to spell some tricky words.

The back part of the dictionary has pages for words you use in different classes, such as science and math classes. These pages are followed by a list of spelling rules, a list of spelling strategies, and a list of words often misspelled. These three lists can help you when you aren't sure how to spell a word.

Enjoy using your dictionary to make words your own.

# Aa

A handsome young man of Spain

Met a lion one day in the rain.

He ran in a fright

With all of his might,

But the lion, he ran with his mane!

Limerick

# Aa

  acorn  antelope  astronaut

able

actually

adjective

already

arrive

A
B
C
D
E
F
G
H
I
J
K
L
M
N
O
P
Q
R
S
T
U
V
W
X
Y
Z

**Memory Jogger**

To remember the *d* in *adjective*, remember that a**d**jectives **d**escribe.

5

# Aa

acorn antelope astronaut

# Aa

 acorn  antelope  astronaut

# Bb

Billy Button bought buttered biscuits.

Buttered biscuits Billy Button bought.

But if Billy Button bought buttered biscuits,

Where are the buttered biscuits

That Billy Button bought?

Tongue Twister

# Bb

 banana     bracelet     buckle

better

billion

break

breathe

business

Memory Jogger

You can see **bus** in **bus**iness.

# Bb

banana  bracelet  buckle

# Bb

banana

bracelet

buckle

# Cc

A canner especially canny

One morning remarked to his granny,

"A canner can can

Anything that he can,

But a canner can't can a can, can he?"

# Cc

cardinal

collie

cylinder

certain

character

chief

clothes

cotton

*Memory Jogger*

To spell *chief,* remember this:
Write *ie* when the sound is long *e,*
except after *c*.

# Cc

cardinal    collie    cylinder

# Cc

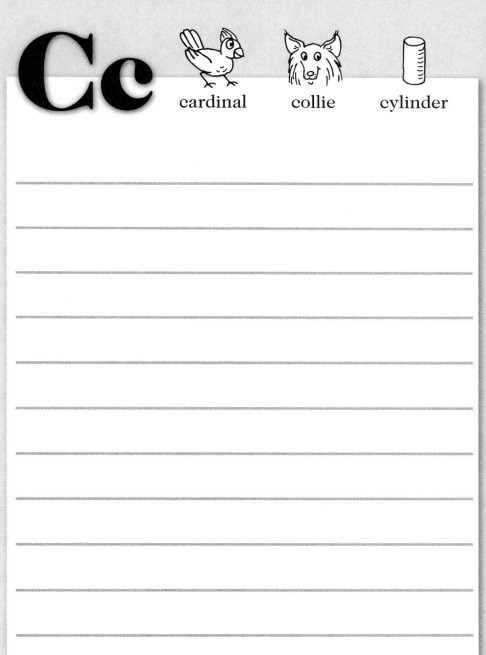

cardinal    collie    cylinder

# Dd

There was an old man of Dumbree

Who taught little owls to drink tea;

For he said, "To eat mice

Is not proper or nice,"

That delightful old man of Dumbree.

Limerick

# Dd

daisy     dessert     dolphin

describe

desert

design

difficult

divide

**Memory Jogger**

To remember how to spell *desert* and *dessert,* remember this: **Two** de**ss**erts are better than **one** de**s**ert.

# Dd

 daisy  dessert  dolphin

# Dd

daisy     dessert     dolphin

# Ee

There was an old man with a beard

Who said, "It is just as I feared!

Two owls and a hen, four larks and a wren

Have all built their nests in my beard!"

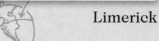

Limerick

# Ee

 eighty

 equator

 eyebrow

either

energy

error

escape

explain

**Memory Jogger**

To spell *explain*, remember this: When you ex**plain** something, you make it **plain.**

21

# Ee

 eighty

 equator

 eyebrow

# Ee

eighty    equator    eyebrow

# Ff

When a jolly young fisher named Fischer

Went fishing for fish in a fissure,

A fish, with a grin,

Pulled the fisherman in.

Now they're fishing the fissure for Fischer.

Limerick

# Ff

 falcon

 faucet

 forty

favorite

foreign

forward

freeze

fruit

Memory Jogger

Say all three syllables of *favorite* to remember the *o*: *fa* **vor** *ite*.

A
B
C
D
E
F
G
H
I
J
K
L
M
N
O
P
Q
R
S
T
U
V
W
X
Y
Z

25

# F f

falcon     faucet     forty

# Ff

falcon      faucet      forty

# Gg

There was a young lady of Greenwich,

Whose garments were bordered with spinach;

But a large spotty calf

Bit her shawl quite in half,

Which alarmed that young lady of Greenwich.

Limerick

# Gg

giraffe

gnaw

graph

garage

germ

glove

group

guard

Memory Jogger

To spell *glove*, remember this sentence: I **love** my new **glove.**

# G g

 giraffe

 gnaw

graph

# Gg

giraffe     gnaw     graph

# Hh

There once was a cowgirl named Harriet,

Who practiced rope tricks with a lariat.

When her horse suddenly stopped,

Harriet's arm quickly dropped,

And the lariat wrapped around Harriet.

Limerick

# Hh

 hamster    helmet    hummingbird

heart

horizon

however

human

hundred

Memory Jogger

You can see **or** and **on** in **horizon**.

# Hh  hamster  helmet  hummingbird

# Hh

 hamster  helmet  hummingbird

# Ii

There's no need to light a night light

On a light night like tonight,

For a night light's light's a slight light

And tonight's a night that's light.

It's really not quite right to light a night light

On a bright-light night like tonight.

Tongue Twister

# Ii

icicle

instrument

ivy

impossible

interest

iron

its

it's

A
B
C
D
E
F
G
H
I
J
K
L
M
N
O
P
Q
R
S
T
U
V
W
X
Y
Z

Memory Jogger

To decide between *it's* and *its*, remember this: *Its* is for owning. *It's* means "it is."

# Ii

icicle    instrument    ivy

# Ii

icicle    instrument    ivy

# Jj

Our Joe wants to know if your Joe

Will lend our Joe your Joe's banjo.

If your Joe will lend our Joe your Joe's banjo,

Our Joe will lend your Joe our Joe's banjo

When our Joe has a banjo!

Tongue Twister

# Jj

jellyfish

jewelry

judge

jealous

join

journey

junior

justice

A
B
C
D
E
F
G
H
I
J
K
L
M
N
O
P
Q
R
S
T
U
V
W
X
Y
Z

Memory Jogger

*Justice = just + ice.*

41

# J j

 jellyfish

 jewelry     judge

# Jj

jellyfish

jewelry

judge

# K k

Old Kate, who had a problem with her trunk,

Wanted to make friends with a skunk.

It worked out quite well,

For Kate couldn't smell

And so couldn't tell that the skunk stunk.

Limerick

# Kk

kettle

keyboard

knight

kangaroo

key

kindness

kitchen

knife

Memory Jogger

Don't forget the *t* in *kitchen*.
Remember that you can see ***kit***
in ***kit***chen.

45

A
B
C
D
E
F
G
H
I
J
**K**
L
M
N
O
P
Q
R
S
T
U
V
W
X
Y
Z

# K k

kettle    keyboard    knight

# Kk

kettle     keyboard     knight

# Ll

There was a young lady from Lynn

Who was so uncommonly thin

That when she strayed

Near a glass of lemonade

She slipped through the straw and fell in.

Limerick

# L l

lettuce    lily    lobster

laughter

length

liquid

listen

locate

Memory Jogger

The le**ng**th of your hair is how lo**ng** it is.

49

# Ll

 lettuce  lily  lobster

# L l

lettuce

lily

lobster

# Mm

A mouse in her room woke Miss Dowd.

She was frightened and screamed very loud.

Then a happy thought hit her—

To scare off the critter,

She sat up in bed and meowed.

Limerick

# Mm

 melon  microscope  moose

material

modern

molecule

moment

myself

Memory Jogger

Remember the **me** in *mo**me**nt*.

# Mm

melon   microscope   moose

# Mm

melon    microscope    moose

# Nn

I need not your needles.

They're needless to me.

But if my neat trousers

Needed new knees,

I would then have need

Of your needles indeed.

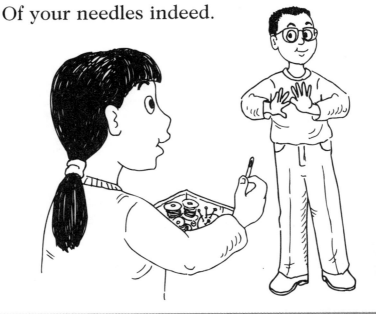

Tongue Twister

# Nn

 napkin

 necklace

 ninety

natural

necessary

noisy

northern

nursery

**Memory Jogger**

To spell *nursery*, remember that a **nurse**ry needs a **nurse**.

# Nn

napkin   necklace   ninety

# Nn

napkin  necklace  ninety

# Oo

A cheerful old bear at the zoo

Could always find something to do.

When it bored him to go

On a walk to and fro,

He reversed it and walked fro and to.

Limerick

# Oo

olive     orangutan     orbit

occur

ocean

opposite

ought

own

Memory Jogger

To spell *occur*, remember that it is like *happen*. The two words have the same meaning. They also have double consonants in the middle.

# Oo

olive    orangutan    orbit

# Oo

olive  orangutan  orbit

# Pp

Peter Piper picked a peck of pickled peppers.

A peck of pickled peppers Peter Piper picked.

If Peter Piper picked a peck of pickled peppers,

How many peppers did Peter Piper pick?

Tongue Twister

# Pp

 penguin     pineapple     pretzel

package

photograph

please

prepare

probably

*Package = pack + age*

# Pp

penguin   pineapple   pretzel

# Pp

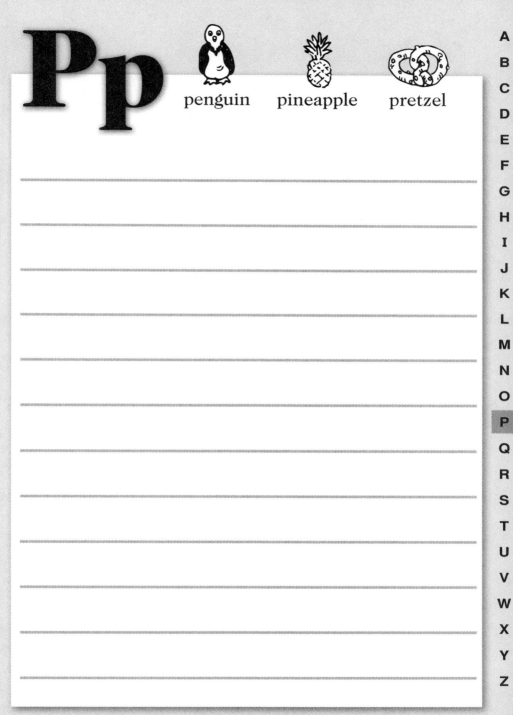

penguin   pineapple   pretzel

# Qq

How many quilts will Queen Quilla quilt

If Queen Quilla quilts quails on quilts?

If Queen Quilla quilts quail quilts quite quickly,

Quite a few quail quilts will Queen Quilla quilt.

Tongue Twister

# Qq

quarter

question

$3\overline{)12}$ ⁴
quotient

quality

quart

quiet

quite

quiver

Memory Jogger

Say *quiet* and *quite* correctly to spell them correctly. *Quiet* has two syllables: **qui • et**. *Quite* has only one.

# Qq

quarter

question

$$3\overline{)12}^{\,4}$$

quotient

# Qq

quarter question quotient

# Rr

A certain young fellow named Robby

Rode his steed back and forth in a lobby.

When the clerk said, "Indoors

Is no place for a horse,"

He replied, "But, you see, it's my hobby!"

Limerick

# Rr

 reptile     rhinoceros     robe

raisin

reason

remember

rough

rhyme

Remember that **rhyme** is like **why**. Both have **hy**.

# Rr

reptile     rhinoceros     robe

# Rr

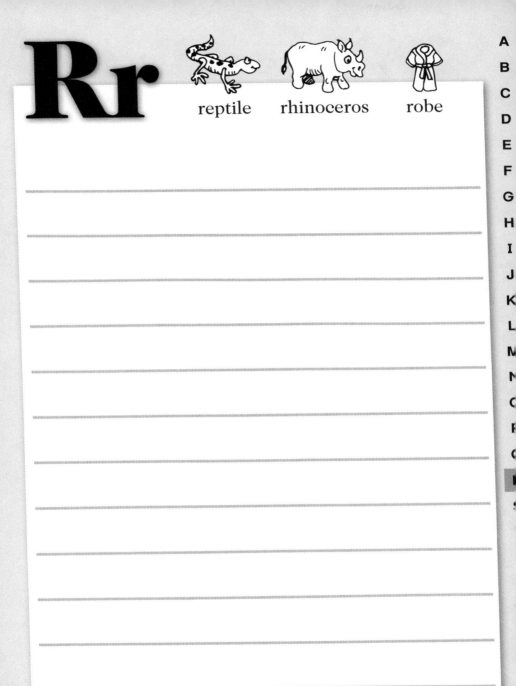

reptile    rhinoceros    robe

# Ss

There once was a snail named Sue

Who wanted to live in a shoe.

A size six was too small,

So she slid down the hall

And found a size twelve with a view.

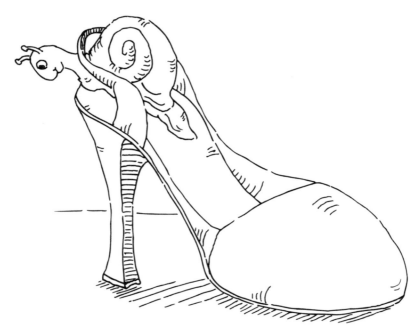

Limerick

# Ss

salmon

serpent

strawberry

Saturday

school

season

shoulder

sugar

Memory Jogger

To spell **Satur**day, remember that it comes from the word **Satur**n. Saturn is the name of a planet and a Roman god of long ago.

# Ss

salmon  serpent  strawberry

# Ss

salmon

serpent

strawberry

# Tt

A tutor who tooted the flute

Tried to tutor two tooters to toot.

Said the two to the tutor,

"Is it harder to toot,

Or to tutor two tooters to toot?"

Limerick

# Tt

tick

toothbrush

triangle

teacher

though

tied

tiny

tongue

Memory Jogger

To spell *teacher*, remember that *teac**her*** has the word **her**.

# T t

tick    toothbrush    triangle

# Tt

tick    toothbrush    triangle

# Uu

There once was a girl named Lou

Who was confused about a beast at the zoo.

She said, "It's true

That I haven't a clue"

And was told, "It's the zoo's new gnu, Lou."

Limerick

# Uu

 unhappy

 uniform

 Utah

uncle

underline

united

unneeded

useful

Memory Jogger

Adding a prefix does not change the spelling of the base word.
**un** + **n**eeded = u**nn**eeded.

# Uu

unhappy

uniform

Utah

# Uu

unhappy     uniform      Utah

# Vv

A hungry young man named Vine,

When asked at what hour he would dine,

Replied, "At eleven,

At three, five, and seven

And eight and a quarter past nine!

Limerick

# Vv

veil

violin

volcano

vacation

valley

various

village

visitor

Memory Jogger

You can see *is*, *it*, and *or* in *vis it or*.

# Vv

veil

violin

volcano

# Vv

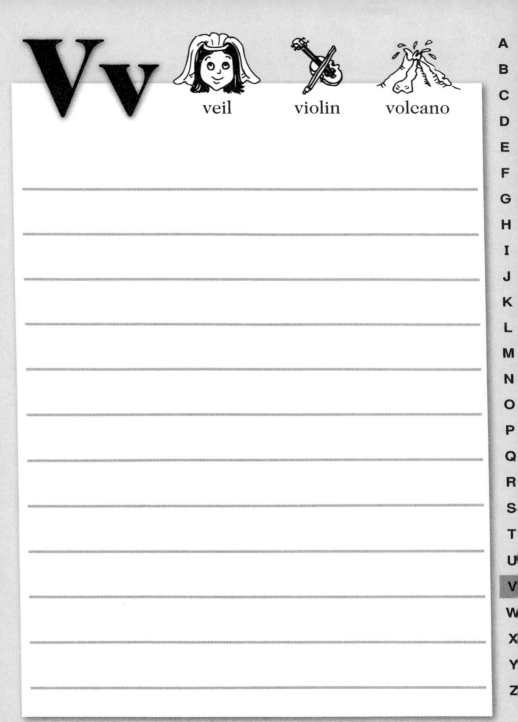

veil    violin    volcano

# Ww

How much wood would a woodchuck chuck

If a woodchuck could chuck wood?

He would chuck, he would, as much as he could.

He would chuck as much as a woodchuck could

If a woodchuck could chuck wood.

Tongue Twister

# Ww

wasp

wheelbarrow

wreath

warm

weird

whether

window

wrinkle

A
B
C
D
E
F
G
H
I
J
K
L
M
N
O
P
Q
R
S
T
U
V
W
X
Y
Z

Memory Jogger

Use this sentence to remember the spelling of *weird*: **We** can remember how to spell **weird**.

# Ww

wasp    wheelbarrow    wreath

# Ww

wasp   wheelbarrow   wreath

There once was an extremely nice ox

Whose best friend in the world was a fox.

When the north wind blew,

The ox knew what to do,

And that's how that fox got his socks.

Limerick

x-ray

xylophone

e<u>x</u>tra

rela<u>x</u>

<u>xy</u>lophone

**Memory Jogger**

The letter pair *xy* often has the sound of *z* at the beginning of a word.

# Yy

There was a young lady of Ealing

Who had a peculiar feeling

That she was a fly

And wanted to try

To walk upside-down on the ceiling.

Limerick

# Yy

yarn

yawn

yolk

A
B
C
D
E
F
G
H
I
J
K
L
M
N
O
P
Q
R
S
T
U
V
W
X
Y
Z

yank

yelp

yesterday

your

you're

**Memory Jogger**

To decide between *you're* and *your*, think about what they are for. *Your* is for owning. *You're* means "you are."

# Zz

Zachary, the zebra at the zoo,

Missed his girlfriend back in Purdue.

He said, "It's not right

To look black and white

When the color you feel is blue."

Limerick

# Zz

zero

zinnia

zipper

zigzag

zip

zone

zoom

Memory Jogger

You can see **zoo** in **zoo**m.

# Social Studies Words

ancient _____    _____

capital _____    _____

continent _____    _____

freedom _____    _____

frontier _____    _____

_____    _____

_____    _____

_____    _____

_____    _____

_____    _____

_____    _____

# Science Words

hatch

leaves

solid

taste

weight

# Math Words

equal

least

order

ray

tenth

# Reading and Language Words

action

audience

describe

paragraph

poem

# Art and Music Words

ballet

carve

clay

orchestra

tune

# Spelling Rules

## Adding Suffixes

Drop the final *e* before adding a suffix that begins with a vowel.

EXAMPLES    close + ing = clos**ing**
use + able = us**able**

Double the final consonant before adding a suffix that begins with a vowel if
1. the word is accented on the last syllable *and*
2. the word ends in a single vowel and a single consonant.

EXAMPLES    plan + ing = plan**n**ing
order + ed = orde**r**ed

EXCEPTIONS  words ending in *w* or *x* — wa**x**ed

For words that end in a consonant and *y*, change *y* to *i* before adding a suffix unless the suffix begins with *i*.

EXAMPLES    empty + ness = empt**iness**
hurry + ing = hurr**ying**

## Adding Prefixes

When adding a prefix to a word, do not change the spelling of the word itself.

EXAMPLES    re + name = **re**name
mis + spell = **mis**spell

## *ie* or *ei*?

**Write *ie* if the sound is long *e*, except after *c*.**

EXAMPLES  p**ie**ce, c**ei**ling, rec**ei**ve

EXCEPTIONS  **ei**ther, w**ei**rd, s**ei**ze

**Write *ei* if the sound is <u>not</u> long *e*, especially if the sound is long *a*.**

EXAMPLES  th**ei**r, v**ei**n, **ei**ght, sl**ei**gh

EXCEPTIONS  p**ie**, fr**ie**nd

## Plurals

**For most nouns, add –*s***

EXAMPLES  dog**s**  pencil**s**  paper**s**
radio**s**  Smith**s**

**For nouns ending in *s*, *x*, *z*, *ch*, or *sh*, add –*es*.**

EXAMPLES  glass**es**  inch**es**
box**es**  Jones**es**

**For nouns ending in a consonant and *y*, change the *y* to *i* and add *es*.**

EXAMPLES  fl**ies**, bab**ies**, lad**ies**

EXCEPTION  proper nouns — the Kell**ys**,
the Darb**ys**

**For nouns ending in a consonant and *o*, add –*es*.**

EXAMPLES  potato**es**, hero**es**

EXCEPTIONS  pianos, solos
proper nouns — the Itos, the Sotos

# Spelling Strategies

1. Say the word. Listen for the consonant and vowel sounds. Think about what the word means.

2. Study the word. Find any prefixes or suffixes that you know. Look for spelling patterns that you know. Think of a rhyming partner—a rhyming word that is spelled the same way. Think of related words.

3. Picture the word in your mind. Spell the word to yourself.

4. Write the word while you look at it.

5. Cover the word. Then write it again. Check your spelling. If you have not spelled the word correctly, practice these steps until you can write it correctly every time.

**If you are not sure how a word is spelled, try these things.**

- Make sure you're pronouncing the word correctly.

- If the word is a compound word, think about how the two shorter words are spelled.

- Think of a rhyming partner that you know how to spell.

- Think of a spelling rule that can help you spell the word.

- Ask an expert.

- Take your best guess. Then check your guess in a dictionary.

- Write the word in a few different ways. Look for the spelling that looks right. Then check the spelling in a dictionary.

# Words Often Misspelled

again

a lot

already

always

and

another

answer

aren't

beautiful

because

before

believe

brought

build

busy

buy

caught

clothes

college

could

decided

didn't

different

doesn't

don't

eight

enough

especially

everybody

everyone

everything

except

excited

eye

family

father

favorite

field

finally

first

friend

friend's

friends

garage

getting

grabbed

great

guess

happened

heard

himself

I'm

into

it's

knee

knew

know

language

laugh

let's

library
live
machine
maybe
measure
million
minute
myself
neighbor
off
often
once
one
our
outside
people
piece
probably
quiet
really
right
rough
said
says

school
science
scissors
should
since
something
sometimes
special
stopped
straight
surprised
that's
their
then
there
there's
they
they're
thought
threw
through
to
tongue
too

tried
until
upon
usually
vacation
vein
want
weather
weight
weird
went
we're
were
what's
when
where
which
whole
whose
woman
wrong
you're